CONTENTS

W9-AOZ-343

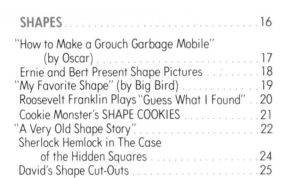

Cookie Monster's Famous Cookie Dough

Dear Reader,

Hello, there! Me COOKIE MONSTER and my favorite thing is EATING COOKIES.

In this book me going to show you how to make ALL KINDS OF COOKIES! But first...me tell you secret recipe for

COOKIE DOUGH (It been in my family for years.)

Here is what you need:

A medium-sized mixing bowl
Measuring cup and spoons
A fork

Butter or margarine (soft, but not melted)

Sugar
2 eggs
Vanilla

All-purpose flour
Baking powder
Salt

What to do to make the dough:

1. Put ¾ cup of butter or margarine (that's a stick and a half) into your mixing bowl.

2. Measure 1 cup of sugar.

3. Pour sugar over butter.

4. With a fork, squash butter and sugar together until they are blended.

5. Crack shells of 2 eggs and pour eggs over mixture in bowl.

6. Measure 1 teaspoon vanilla and pour over mixture.

7. With fork, blend everything in the bowl together.

8. Measure 2½ cups of all-purpose flour and pour over mixture in bowl.

9. Measure 1 teaspoon baking powder and sprinkle over flour.

10. Measure 1 teaspoon salt and sprinkle over flour and baking powder.

11. Mix everything together either with the fork or with your hands.

12. Put dough in icebox to chill (at least one hour).

You can make LOTS of dough at once and keep it in your icebox in a plastic bag (it will last a long time). Then whenever you make COOKIES, just take out as much as you need.

In MY house it no last very long at all. HAPPY COOKIE MAKING!

Love,

Cookie

Here are some of the people
who helped me with my BUSY BOOK...

Chief Photo Researcher:
> Geraldine Hennessey

Photographers:
> Bob Fuhring
> Bill Pierce
> Judy Ross

Chief Cookie Researcher:
> Linda Ortlieb

Chief Magician's Assistant:
> Rollie Krewson

Box Town Builders and Contractors:
> Calley
> Christina
> and
> Jonathan Frith

Chief Cutter and Paster:
> Armando J. Pitaro

Editorial Assistance:
> Eleanor Ehrhardt
> Sue Tarsky
> Anna Jane Hays

And the BUSIEST Person in My Neighborhood
ELMA OTTO

Thank you all very very much.

Love,

BIG BIRD

BIG BIRD'S BUSY BOOK

STARRING
JIM HENSON'S MUPPETS

By
MICHAEL FRITH and SHARON LERNER

special material by
Emily Perl Kingsley and Nina B. Link

Illustrated By
MEL CRAWFORD   A. DELANEY
MICHAEL FRITH   DAVE GANTZ
JON McINTOSH   JOSEPH MATHIEU
CAROLL SPINNEY

with
Carla Bauer   Carol Nicklaus

Special Photography By
CHARLES ROWAN

Welcome to my BUSY BOOK! It's a WONDERFUL PLACE TO BE! It's full of things to MAKE and DO, and *lots* of pictures of ME!

SAVE YOUR JUNK
by O.T. Grouch

Dear Reader ...

It has come to my attention that SOME OF YOU have been throwing away valuable TRASH! Well, STOP! We GrouchEs never throw away ANY-THING- becAuse there are all Kinds of things you can MAKE out of trash. Now, here's my list of imPORTANT JUNK that I like to save.

Old newspapers and
Magazines
Egg cartons
Paper bags
Brown wrapping paper
Cardboard tubes
Pieces of cardboard
CardboArd boxes
(Shoe , cereal, etc)
Cups and paper plates
Milk and juice carTons
coat hangers
Buttons
Paper clips
Thread
Spools
Bottle caps
Popsicle sticks

old socks
Yarn/ ribbon
and string
TiN foil scraps
corKs
straws
Bleach bottles and
other plastic
bottles
Juice cans
cloth scraps
Jars & lids
pins
eyeglasses
old ping-pong balls
rubber bands

Boy! Look at all that great stuff! Now, will you Do me a Favor? TURN THE PAGE and LEAVE ME ALONE !.

GROuchily Yours,

OSCAR
BAH!

P.S. (by Big Bird)
Gee, you know, that really IS a great list. And they're all things you can use in my BUSY BOOK. You'll also need:

Crayons
Pencils
Glue or paste
Paper
Scissors

Tape
Pipe cleaners
Paint
Food coloring

Have fun!
Love,
BIGBIRD

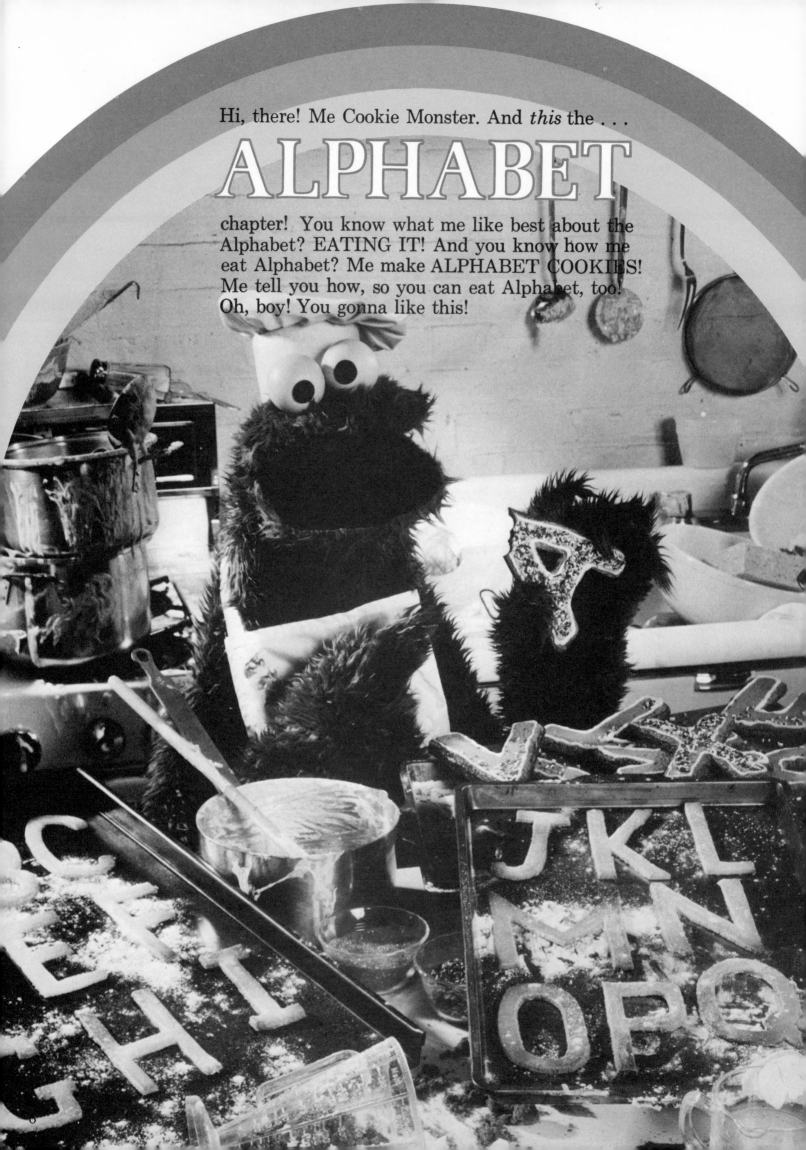

Hi, there! Me Cookie Monster. And *this* the . . .

ALPHABET

chapter! You know what me like best about the Alphabet? EATING IT! And you know how me eat Alphabet? Me make ALPHABET COOKIES! Me tell you how, so you can eat Alphabet, too! Oh, boy! You gonna like this!

Cookie Monster's Alphabet Cookies

First you need to make cookie dough! If you look at page 4, it will tell you all about how to do that. O.K., cookie dough ready? Here we go!

1. Heat oven to 400 degrees.

2. Put cloth on table. Sprinkle with flour.

3. Roll out dough on cloth, about ¼ inch thick.

4. Cut dough into strips.

5. Use strips of dough to make your FAVORITE letters.

A B C D E F G H I J K L M N O P Q R S T U V W X Y Z

6. Put cookie letters on ungreased cookie sheet.

7. O.K. Now comes HARDEST part of all ... Put in oven and WAIT six to eight minutes. OH ... ME hate this waiting around ... Me have little snack while me wait ...

TABLE! (Yum, yum!)
CHAIR! (Munch, crunch)

POTS! PANS! ROLLING PIN! (Oh, boy! Gobble) EGGBEATER! SINK! (Oof, Umf)

Hey, me think cookies about ready now ... just in time for dessert.

Boy, that sure was a good sink ...

Snuffie Learns the Alphabet
by Big Bird

When Mr. Snuffle-upagus
was just a little kid
He had a great big problem,
And this is what he did.
He came one day and said to me,
"I've found this big, long word.
I don't know how to say it, though—
Can you explain it, Bird?"

I took that piece of paper,
I looked at it and smiled,
"I used to make the same mistake
When I was just a child.

"This thing is not a word at all—
It's called the ALPHABET.
Just say each letter separately,
And *this* is what you'll get . . ."

O.K., now, say this along with me, and we'll teach Mr. Snuffle-upagus how the Alphabet goes.

ABCD...EFG
HIJK...LMNOP
QRS...TUV
WX...Y...Z

"I think that you know
EVERYTHING,"
I heard my friend Snuff say.
"When did *you* learn the
Alphabet?"

Oh . . . I learned it yesterday.

Ernie and the Letter M

One day, when Ernie was eating his lunch
in the park, he heard a mysterious voice...

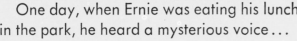

Hey...
KID!

Who...
ME?

Sshhhhhh! Not so loud.
How'd ya like t'buy this
terrific... LETTER **M**?

A letter **M**?
What would I ever do
with a letter **M**?

Well... suppose ya want to put some
MUSTARD on that sandwich and
y'wanna know what letter **M**USTARD
begins with. Well... ya just
look at yer letter **M**...
and there ya have it!

But I don't *like*
mustard on peanut butter
sandwiches!

Ya *don't?* Well,
suppose you were about ta
have a glass of that **M**ILK,
and ya wanted to know
what letter **M**ILK begins
with. Ya just take out
yer letter **M**...

But
I'm having
orange juice
for lunch.

Ya are? Well, how about dessert! I'll bet
ya have some nice **M**ARSHMALLOWS in there...   Nope.
MACAROONS?   Nope.
MUFFINS with **M**ARMALADE?   Nope.
MARBLE CAKE?   Nope.

A **M**ALTED?
MAPLE sugar?
MACADAMIA nuts?

Nope.
Nope.
Nope.

O.K. I give up.
What ARE ya havin'
for dessert?

This nice...
big... fat...
WATERMELON!

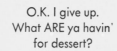

A **W**ATERMELON?

WATERMELON
starts with
W!

Hey, kid...
How'd ya like to buy
this terrific...
LETTER **W**?

Hey, it's me, Oscar the Grouch! Now, if you'll give me a nice big frown, I'll show you something I just made. It's my

Grouch Alphabet Book

I looked through all the magazines in my trash collection, cut out the GROUCHY pictures, and pasted them in.

Aa
An Angry Alligator
An Apple core

Bb
A Broken Bottle
A Bawling Baby

Oh, Oscar, I made an Alphabet Book, too, but I call it "Betty Lou's Lovely Letter Book." Here are two of *my* favorite pages.

Cc

a cuddly cub

a candy cane

Dd

a darling doggie

a dozen dandelions

If you want to make a book like mine, here's how to do it. First, find 14 pieces of paper.

Write your name on the first page. Then, using both sides of the paper, write a letter of the alphabet near the top of each of the other pages.

Now look through your old magazines and newspapers and cut out pictures of things that start with each letter.

Stick the things that start with A on the A page, and the B things on the B page, and so on.

If you can't find a picture you like, you can draw one yourself.

Put all the pages together, like a book. Punch two holes in the side, like this.

Then, find some pretty ribbon or yarn, put it through the holes, and tie a bow. Then you'll have your very *own* "Lovely Letter Book."

Yucch! That's what I call a LOUSY letter book! Now, look at this...here are some mad monkeys munching on moldy marshmallows, and...

a b c d e f g h i j k l m n o p q r s t u v w x y z

Sherlock Hemlock in The Mystery of the Missing Alphabet

Oh, Mr. Hemlock!
I was teaching Mr. Snuffle-upagus
the ALPHABET and he SNEEZED and
blew all the letters all over the STREET
and now I can't find them!
Whatever shall we do!

E-GAD!
The WHOLE
alphabet . . . MISSING!
This sounds like a job
for Sherlock Hemlock, the
World's Greatest
Detective!

Hmmmmmmm. This may be harder than I thought. Perhaps you will help me by taking your crayons and coloring in all the letters, from A to Z. ZOUNDS! We'll solve this case yet!

Did you find ALL the letters? Turn the page and see.

The Grouch Garbage MOBILE

What you need

1. Wire coat hanger.
2. Tin foil or yarn.
3. String.
4. Different-shaped things:
   Circles—bottle caps, buttons.
   Squares—paper napkins, small empty boxes and box tops.

   Triangles—bobby pins, paper clips, straws, or pipe cleaners, bent into triangles.
   Other shapes—cardboard cutouts, cookie cutters.

What you do

Ernie and Bert Present...
Shape Pictures

Ernie, I have the square, the triangle, and the rectangle. All you had to get was the circle.

How can we make shape pictures if you don't have the circle?

Bert and Ernie are proud to present SHAPE PICTURES!

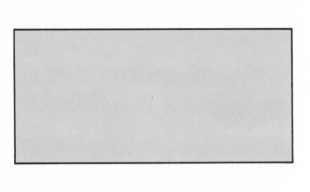

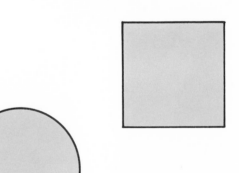

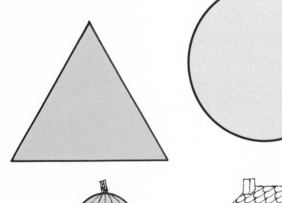

Here are some pictures we made out of these shapes... And here are some extra shapes for YOU to make pictures out of. That triangle might make a *nifty* pigeon...

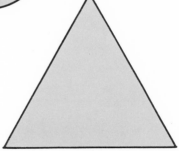

Hey, Berd... cad I hab by dose bag dow?

18

My Favorite SHAPE!
by Big Bird

The CIRCLE is my favorite shape,
And I will tell you why.
Because it's the shape
Of my FAV-OR-ITE food—
A crunchy birdseed pie!

But...
I mustn't forget the RECTANGLE—
I like *that* best by far.
'Cause that's the shape
Of a *chocolate-covered*
Birdseed candy bar.

But, WAIT! I forgot about TRIANGLES!
Triangles are VERY nice.
Like a piece of birdseed pizza.
Please—can I have a slice?

Oh, no! I can't leave out the SQUARE...
I love that shape the most.
When bedtime comes I always have
Some milk and birdseed toast.

I guess it doesn't matter
If it's round or if it's square—
ALL shapes are really tasty,
So long as BIRDSEED's there.

Hi! I'm Roosevelt Franklin and I really know my shapes. Here's a groovy game about shapes. It's called

GUESS WHAT I FOUND

First, get some friends to play with you. Then look around the room and choose something square, like a box or that windowpane. Don't say the name of the thing, but shout out, "Hey, I looked around, and guess what I found. I found something . . . *square!*"

Your friends have to try to guess what it is. They say . . .

Cookie Monster's Shape Cookies

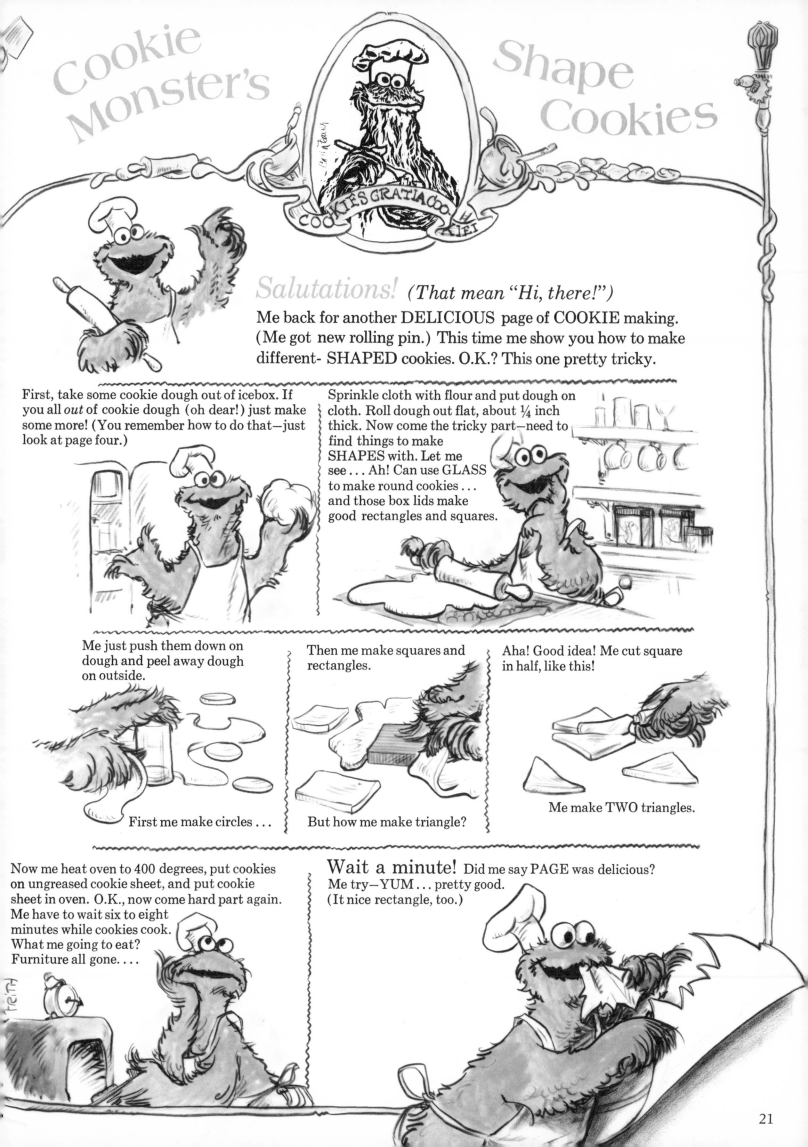

Salutations! *(That mean "Hi, there!")*

Me back for another DELICIOUS page of COOKIE making. (Me got new rolling pin.) This time me show you how to make different-SHAPED cookies. O.K.? This one pretty tricky.

First, take some cookie dough out of icebox. If you all *out* of cookie dough (oh dear!) just make some more! (You remember how to do that—just look at page four.)

Sprinkle cloth with flour and put dough on cloth. Roll dough out flat, about ¼ inch thick. Now come the tricky part—need to find things to make SHAPES with. Let me see . . . Ah! Can use GLASS to make round cookies . . . and those box lids make good rectangles and squares.

Me just push them down on dough and peel away dough on outside.

First me make circles . . .

Then me make squares and rectangles.

But how me make triangle?

Aha! Good idea! Me cut square in half, like this!

Me make TWO triangles.

Now me heat oven to 400 degrees, put cookies on ungreased cookie sheet, and put cookie sheet in oven. O.K., now come hard part again. Me have to wait six to eight minutes while cookies cook. What me going to eat? Furniture all gone. . . .

Wait a minute! Did me say PAGE was delicious? Me try—YUM . . . pretty good. (It nice rectangle, too.)

A Very Old Shape Story

One day, a very long time ago, a cave man was pulling a box of rocks. "This rock box is so hard to pull," the cave man complained, "that by the time I get to my rock garden I'm too tired to do anything."

Then the cave man had a terrific idea. "I'll put some things under the rock box to make it roll," he shouted out.

He went to his cave. Since triangles were his favorite shape, he decided to use triangles. After many hours of hard work, the cave man had hammered out four stone triangles. He attached them to his rock box and began to pull. Because the triangles had three corners, they couldn't roll.

He pulled

and pulled...

until...

the rope broke.

"I really do love triangles, but maybe I'd better use squares instead," he thought to himself. So he went back to the cave and hammered out four stone squares.

He attached them to his rock box and pulled. The squares were even harder to pull than the triangles because they had four corners. Again the rope broke.

"I guess this wasn't such a hot idea," the cave man mumbled as he kicked a big round rock sitting in his path. The round rock began to roll down the hill.

"Round!" the cave man yelled. "Why didn't I think of that before?"

So he hurried home and hammered out four round stones. When he attached them to his rock box the round stones rolled smoothly along because they didn't have any corners.

Pretty soon all his neighbors wanted round stones for their rock boxes, too, so the cave man opened up a Round Stone Shop in his cave. "I think I'll call these round stones...*bananas*," the cave man announced—and so he did.

The End

23

Sherlock Hemlock in
The Case of the Hidden Squares

I, Sherlock Hemlock, the World's Greatest Detective, have found 16 squares in this picture. Can you find that many? Color them and see.

Hey, look at that! That ice-cream cone looks sort of like a triangle and a circle put together. You know, you can make a lot of things out of shapes.

Just trace these shapes... or draw your own and cut them out.

...And here are some of the things you can make... Now see what *you* can do.

I, Grover, am here to present
the
NATURE
chapter.

Oh, I am so proud!

Crafts for All Seasons

Spring

Hello, everybodee! This is Old Farmer Grover here. It is springtime, and spring is the time when all the pretty flowers bloom. I will show you how to make some flowers of your own.

Get some paper cups, some straws, some paste, and some paper and crayons. Draw some BEAUTIFUL flowers on the paper, cut them out, and stick them to the straws. Then put some sand in the cups and stick the straws in the sand. AREN'T THEY BEAUTIFUL?

You can even decorate the cups, like I did.

Use Paste or Tape

Summer

You know what us Grouches like to do in the summer? We like to go down to the *swamp* and play in the MUD. Here are some of my favorite MUD toys...

The best thing to use is a plastic bleach bottle. You can cut off the bottom, and use it for a pail.

And you can cut the top, like this... and it makes a super-dooper *mud* scooper.

Of course, if you're not a grouch you can use them at the beach for SAND toys...
.....BLECCH!

KNEE DEEP!

Fall

Hi, I'm Betty Lou. When the fall winds blow, I love to make pretty pinwheels and watch them spin. First, take a square piece of paper and color it with bright designs on both sides.

Then fold it in half, like this...

and then again, like this...

Now draw a small circle right in the middle of the paper. Cut on the fold lines toward the middle, until you reach the outside of your circle. BE SURE you don't cut all the way through the middle.

Now take one corner of each triangle and stick it to your middle circle like this...

Last of all, take a pin and a straw, and stick the pin through the middle of the pinwheel and through the straw.

(Stick a piece of cork or the eraser from a pencil on the pin so you won't get pricked.)

Now you can take your pinwheel out for a spin.

Winter

Oh, dear! It's getting cold. It must be winter. Do you know what I love about the winter? All the beautiful snowflakes. I'll show you how to make some. All you need is some white paper squares and a pair of scissors.

First fold your paper in half. Then fold it in half again... and then fold it one MORE time, into a triangle.

Now snip out bits from each side of the triangle.

Be sure to leave some space between each snip.

You can make all different kinds of snowflakes to hang on your walls and windows. Isn't that nice?

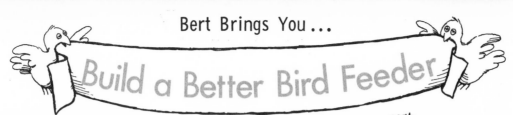

Build a Better Bird Feeder

Hello! Welcome! Welcome to the weekly meeting of the Sesame Street Pigeon Lovers Club. This week we are going to talk about making a bird feeder for ALL our feathered friends.

Making a bird feeder is easy. All you need is an empty milk carton. First, have someone cut a hole in it, like this.

Punch a hole in the top and tie a piece of string to it.

Put some birdseed or bread crumbs in it and hang it up on a tree, or a fire escape, or out your window. Then you can watch the little birdies in your neighborhood as they hop in and out of your milk carton bird feeder looking for their supper.

Of course, in OUR neighborhood we have to do things a little differently ...

J. Mathieu

A Rain Poem

I love the rain because the flowers
All need the rain to help them grow.
I sit inside and watch for hours,
And I don't mind because I know
The daffodils outside the windowpane
Agree with me—and really love the rain.

What a dumb reason to love the rain!

I love it when it pours down without stopping
'Cause everyone gets *soaked* from head to toe.
Their hair gets wet, their shoes
 and socks are sopping,
They step in puddles everywhere they go.

Listen to those people all complain (heh, heh)—
And *that* is why us Grouches love the rain.

Look out! Here comes a taxi!
Oh! That was beautiful!

I love the rain...and when the raindrops
Fall so softly from the sky,
I go outside with my umbrella
And COUNT THEM as they're dropping by.
And the reason that I really love them
Is because there are so many of them.
Ha, ha, ha!

WONDERFUL!
WONDERFUL!

We all love the rain for different reasons—
It doesn't matter that we don't agree,
For something that is wonderful to you, friend,
May be something else entirely to me.

So if I love the rain because of flowers...

And soggy things and mud
just make me sing...

And I could count the drops
that fall for hours...

We all agree at least on one small thing—
We love the rain!

A Twiddle-Butterfly

Colored by _____

Sherlock Hemlock
in
The Case of the Missing Caterpillar
or
THE CLUE OF THE CRACKED COCOON

What seems to be the trouble, my furry blue friend?

(sniff) My little fuzzy pet caterpillar, Clarence, is missing! Oh, whatever shall I do?

Egad! Missing! This looks like a job for the World's Greatest Detective!

And who might that be?

It is I! Sherlock Hemlock! Now, the first thing we must do is look for clues. Hmmmmm. Are there any caterpillar footprints about?

No. But there is a funny little thing hanging on Clarence's favorite leaf.

Look! There is a funny little thing hanging on Clarence's favorite leaf! Why, it looks like . . . a cracked cocoon!

Oh, Mr. Detective! What is a cocoon?

Well, Grover, when a caterpillar reaches a certain age it makes a cocoon around itself. Inside the cocoon a mysterious thing happens. The caterpillar slowly turns into . . . a butterfly!

33

Then it cracks open the cocoon and flies away. This cracked cocoon means that Clarence is now a butterfly! I, Sherlock Hemlock, have solved another case! Why, young man, why are you crying again?

Oh, Mr. Detective! Clarence, my pet *butterfly*, is missing! Whatever shall I do?

Never fear! I, Sherlock Hemlock, will solve the case. Pardon me, sir. Is your name Clarence? Excuse me, madam. Are you Clarence? I beg your pardon . . .

Ernie Plants a Garden

Cookie Monster's Butterfly Cookies

What? You hungry again? Well... YOU IN LUCK! It time to make
BUTTERFLY COOKIES.

First, get out your dough. What? You need more?
O.K. Turn back to page four and make some.

Ready now? We going to make some COOKIE PAINT!

1. First get some evaporated milk
(or mix 1 egg yolk with ¼ teaspoon of water).
Then get some cups and put a little milk or
egg mixture in each one.

2. Now add some food coloring to each cup. You get
COOKIE PAINT! If paint gets too thick, just
add a few drops of water.

Now sprinkle cloth with flour and roll out dough on it, about ¼ inch thick.

Cut little strip of dough for middle of butterfly.

Next come wings—You remember how to make circle cookies? Just press down glass and peel away extra dough.

Then cut circle in half . . .

Now put pieces together like this . . .

And PAINT with your pretty cookie paint . . . and you have a BEAUTIFUL butterfly.

Now heat oven to 400 degrees. Put butterflies on ungreased cookie sheet and COOK 6 to 8 minutes.

Now what we do while butterflies cook?

ME KNOW!

We can play game on next page.

Do you know where all the GOOD THINGS that go into Cookie Monster's FAMOUS COOKIE DOUGH come from? Well, you gonna find out now! Just follow the paths.

FLOUR comes from WHEAT that grows in a field.

EGGS come from CHICKENS.

BUTTER comes from MILK, and milk comes from COWS.

Most SUGAR comes from a plant called SUGAR CANE.

O.K., me think butterflies are ready now. Me look...

Oh, NO! Come back! Oh! This is TERRIBLE!

And Now I,
The Amazing Mumford,
Present...

COLORS

Roosevelt Franklin Plays
GUESS WHAT I FOUND

Remember that groovy game Roosevelt Franklin taught you, called GUESS WHAT I FOUND? You won't believe this, but you can play that <u>same game</u> using colors. Too much!

The first player looks around, chooses something red, and says, "I looked around, and guess what I found. I found something red." He might choose a red book, or a red pencil, or even somebody's red shirt.

The other players try to guess what he found. The one who guesses right gets to choose the next color...like, "I looked around, and guess what I found. I found something YELLOW." Out of sight!

Roosevelt Franklin sure likes this game! You just keep on playing until you've used up all of the colors you can. Then you can start all over again.

Here are some good colors to look for.

red   green   blue   yellow

Oscar's Trash Can Crayon Holder

I always used to lose my crayons in all the junk here in my trash can—so I made a separate little trash can just for them.

Here's how you can make one, too.

First, Take some scissors and cut along that dotted line.

Second, Get an old juice can (make sure it doesn't have any sharp edges).

Third, Wrap the trash can picture around it. Glue or tape the picture to the can.

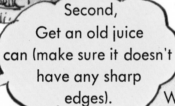

That's it. Pretty neat, huh?

CRAYONS

PENCILS

Big Bird's COLORS

GREEN is the color of Granny Bird's couch, of grass and of spinach and Oscar the Grouch.

It's not easy being green.

Cookie and Grover and Herry are **BLUE**, and bluebirds and bluebells and blueberries, too.

Do you prefer the gold or silver trim?

This flower is **PURPLE** and so are these grapes, and so are ALL of Prince Charming's fine capes.

RED is tomatoes, stoplights and cherries, and strawberry jam— and that necktie of Herry's!

An orange is **ORANGE** and so is Bert's nose— and Ernie is orange—and so are my toes.

YELLOW bananas—and a big bumblebee, and daisies and butter —and don't forget ME!

Cookie Monster's Colored Candy Cookies

COOKIES GRATIA COOKIET

Oh, boy! Me got a good one for you this time! COLORED CANDY COOKIES! They not only *delicious*, they *beautiful*, too! For this one you need:

1. Your COOKIE DOUGH! If you no have some in icebox, make some, QUICK! (See page four.)

2. Some lollipops or hard candies. Find some pretty colored ones.

3. Hammer (or something to break up candies with).

4. Tin foil.

Cover cookie sheet with tin foil. Sprinkle flour on cloth. Roll out dough on cloth (about ¼ inch thick) and cut into thin strips. Now use strips of dough to make pictures on tin foil, like this . . .

Now break up colored candies into little pieces and put pieces in openings in your pictures, like this . . .

Now bake 6 to 8 minutes. While me wait, me play Roosevelt Franklin's favorite game. Hmmm. Me look around, and guess what me found. It something RED and . . . TASTY—

COOK BOOK! Yum, yum, *yum.*

O.K. COOKIES READY!

If you want to make beautiful COOKIE-POPS, put sticks in while still hot. Then let cool and peel off tin foil when hard. Oh, they ALMOST too pretty to eat.

But not quite!

The Story of Princess Ruby

One day Princess Ruby was out in the garden painting a
picture of her Royal roses. Just as she was painting the last
rose petal, a fox jumped out from behind a rose bush.
Princess Ruby was so startled that she tripped over her chair
and fell right into the bucket of red paint. She had red paint
in her hair, red paint in her ears, and red paint all over her
Royal overalls. She was a mess.

"Blecch!" said Princess Ruby. "I will have to take a bath—and
I've already *had* one today! Oh, I *hate* the color red!"

Princess Ruby went upstairs to the Royal bathtub. Her
mother, Queen Rosalie, took the Royal scrub brush and began
to scrub the Princess. It took an hour to scrub the red paint
off her Royal face. It took another hour to scrub the red
paint out of her Royal hair. It took two more hours to scrub
the red paint out of her Royal ears. And worst of all, her favorite
pair of Royal overalls was ruined!

"Red, red, red! I *hate* the color red! I never want to see the color
red again! Mother," she said, "I want you to issue a Proclamation.
Tell *everyone* in the Kingdom to get rid of EVERYTHING that's red!"

Queen Rosalie, who always tried to please her daughter, said, "All right, dear. But are you sure that's what you want?"

"Absolutely!" shouted Princess Ruby. And so the Queen ordered everyone in the Kingdom to get rid of EVERYTHING that was red.

By now it was dinner time, and Princess Ruby was hungry. She went down to the Royal kitchen and spoke to the Royal cook.

"Royal Cook," she said, "I'm hungry. Make me my favorite sandwich—peanut butter and strawberry jam."

"I am so sorry, Your Highness," said the Royal cook, "but there is no strawberry jam. The Proclamation said we had to get rid of EVERYTHING red, and strawberry jam is red. So out it went! You will have to have peanut butter and mint jelly."

"Yucch!" said the Princess. "Mint jelly is green and disgusting. I *hate* mint jelly."

But that was all there was, so that was what she had.

After dinner it was time for the Princess to go to bed. "Royal Mommy," she said to Queen Rosalie, "will you please read me my favorite bedtime story?"

"Of course, dear," said the Queen. "Which one is that?"

"Oh," said Princess Ruby, "it's the one about the little girl who carries a basket of goodies through the woods to her grandmother's house."

"You mean 'Little Red Riding Hood'?" said the Queen. "We don't have that one any more. You wanted us to get rid of EVERYTHING red, so we had to throw it away. I'll have to read 'Little Boy Blue' instead."

"Aaaacch!" groaned the Princess. "I HATE that story!"

But that was all there was, so that was what she had.

The next day was Valentine's Day, Princess Ruby's favorite day of the year. She LOVED to get valentines. And since everyone in the Kingdom loved *her*, she always got a great many valentines. So, bright and early that morning, she ran down the path to meet the Royal mailman.

"Good morning, Royal Mailman," she said. "May I have my valentines, please?"

"Sorry, Princess," said the mailman, "but valentines are red, and the Proclamation said we had to get rid of EVERYTHING red. So I sent all the valentines to my aunt in Peoria. You'll have to go back and look at that Get Well card I brought you when you had the flu."

"That does it!" yelled the Princess. "Royal Mommy! Royal Mommy! Quick—we need another Proclamation."

"I thought we might," said the Queen, smiling. "I have one right here. I hereby proclaim that the color red is allowed back in the Kingdom!"

And right away, the mailman called his aunt in Peoria and she sent back ALL of Princess Ruby's valentines, AND a big jar of homemade strawberry jam, AND a brand-new copy of "Little Red Riding Hood." And that night, after Ruby had looked at all her valentines and eaten two big peanut butter and strawberry jam sandwiches, and Queen Rosalie had read "Little Red Riding Hood" to her twice, she looked up at her Royal Mommy and said, "Royal Mommy, I've really learned a lesson today. Red is a very important color. My favorite food has red in it, and my favorite story has red in it, and my favorite holiday wouldn't be the same without the color red. In fact, red is my favorite color. From now on I will wear only red overalls, and I will eat only red food, and I only want to hear stories about red things, and I want my room painted red. In fact, I want the whole palace painted red, and..."

Queen Rosalie leaned over, kissed her daughter on the forehead, and said softly, "Yes, dear. Go to sleep now, and we'll talk about it in the morning."

Hello! Hello! Welcome to our show! This is GUY SMILEY, everybody's FAVORITE game show host, and it's time for THE

RAINBOW RACE

First, each of you chooses a color on the rainbow. Then you each find a button or a penny or some small marker and put it on the first square of that color.

Next, cut out the four colored squares at the bottom of this page and put them in a paper bag.

O.K. Now the first player reaches into the paper bag (don't peek), and pulls out . . . A COLORED SQUARE! If you get YOUR rainbow color, you can move your marker ONE SQUARE ahead. If you don't get your color, stay where you are. REMEMBER TO PUT THE SQUARE BACK IN THE BAG AFTER EACH TURN! The first one to reach THE GREAT JAR OF JELLYBEANS at the end of the rainbow . . . WINS!!!

Have fun and . . .   GOOD LUCK   on your RAINBOW RACE!

START

FINISH

red

yellow

green

blue

Extra Markers

47

PEOPLE
IN YOUR
NEIGHBORHOOD

(Brought to you by Bert)

Bert's Box Town Neighborhood

Boy, am I proud of this . . . I made a box town for my friends, the Twiddlebugs. I've been collecting these nifty boxes for a long time. I guess you could find boxes of every shape in the whole world in my box town. If you want to collect boxes, then you can make a Twiddlebug box town, too.

What you'll need:

Boxes of all different shapes. Cereal boxes, oatmeal boxes, shoe boxes, milk and juice cartons, spaghetti boxes, etc.

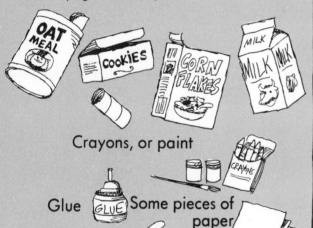

Crayons, or paint

Glue

Some pieces of paper

Scissors

What you do:

1. With paper, and crayons or paint, decorate boxes to look like houses and stores.

2. Cut doors that open and close in the houses and stores.

3. You can even glue boxes one on top of another to make some apartment houses.

4. Cut out the signs and Twiddlebug pictures and paste them on the boxes.

5. You can use toy cars in your town, too.

POLICE STATION

Bakery

Fire Station

DOCTOR BUG M.D.
Specialist
WINGS & FEELERS

GROCER

Grover's Neighborhood Games

Hello, everybodeeee!

I, Grover have a wonderful new GUESSING GAME for Big Bird's Busy Book.

You pretend you are a person who works in your neighborhood and act out your job. See if your friends can guess who you are.

When I play, I pretend to put out a big fire with a hose.

Can you guess who I am?

Did you say a *fireman*?

Ooooh! You are SO SMART!

Sometimes I like to dress up like different people in the neighborhood. Here are some of my FAVORITE costumes.

GROVER THE MAILMAN—Make a mail bag for your letters out of a paper folder. Use cardboard or construction paper to make a hat.

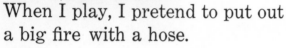

GROVER THE POLICEMAN—Cover a round piece of cardboard with silver foil for a badge. Make a police hat out of cardboard.

GROVER THE DOCTOR—Hang a spool of thread around your neck on a string for a stethoscope. An old shoe box can be your doctor's bag. Fill it with empty bottles and bandages made out of some clean rags.

All right, now—open wide. Say "Aaaahhh . . ." Oh, what cute tonsils you have!

The People in Your Neighborhood

Hi, everybody.
Who are you?

We're People in Your
Neighborhood.
See if you can guess which
ones we are.

Does your bathtub need repairing?
Is there something in your drain?
Do you have a leaky faucet
That is driving you insane?
Don't call up a policeman—
    that's as silly as can be.
For fixing leaks and tubs and
    drains
The one to call is ME!
        I am the _ _ _ _ _ _ _.

When your hair's so long and shaggy
That you bump into a tree,
When you can't see where you're going—
Then it's time to come see ME!
I will cut your hair and comb it,
And I'll make you look so good
That I'll be your very favorite Person
In Your Neighborhood!
        I am the _ _ _ _ _ _.

When you come into my office
First you sit down in my chair,
Then you open up your mouth
So I can see the teeth in there.
First I count them—
Then I clean them,
And I see if they're all right,
And I tell you to please brush them
In the morning and at night!
        I am the _ _ _ _ _ _ _.

PLUMBER DENTIST BARBER

Sam the Shoemaker

One day Maria was walking down the street when she met Sam the Robot. "Where are you going?" Sam asked. "To the shoemaker," Maria answered. "The heel came off my shoe and I have to wear it tonight. And I need to have my shoes shined, too."
"I will fix your shoe," said Sam. "I am a machine. I am perfect. I can do anything."
Maria thought for a minute. She had always taken her shoes to the shoemaker to be fixed. But she didn't want to hurt Sam's feelings, so she dropped her shoe into Sam's hatch.

Bells rang! Lights flashed! And from deep inside Sam came strange whirring and hammering noises.
"Your shoe is now fixed," Sam said, and his hatch popped open.
Maria pulled out her shoe. She looked at it. "Sam," she said, "I'm afraid you made a mistake. You put the heel on the front of the shoe instead of on the back. Maybe I'll just go to the shoemaker and he'll..."

"Wait!" said Sam. "I will fix your shoe. I am perfect. I will put the heel in the right place!"
Maria dropped the shoe back in and the lights started flashing again.

But this time when Sam was finished, he had put the heel in the *middle* of the shoe. "Sam," Maria tried to explain as she held up her other shoe (the one with the heel in the right place), "Sam, don't you see? These two shoes have to be *exactly* the same."

"I can do anything," said Sam. "Give me the two shoes."
Maria put the two shoes in the hatch and waited. And this time, when the hatch opened, both shoes *were* exactly the same...

They *both* had heels in the middle.
"Sam," cried Maria, "what have you done to my shoes?"
"I have made them both the same," Sam explained. "Maria, where are you going? I have not shined your shoes yet."
"To the shoemaker!" Maria yelled as she ran down the street. "Now I've got to have *both* my shoes fixed."

Cookie and the Count LOVE the Baker

Greetings!
I am **the Count.**
My favorite person in the neighborhood is the baker. Do you know why I love the baker? Because he bakes many cookies. And **I love** to *count* cookies.

Howdy!
Me **Cookie Monster.**
And my favorite person in neighborhood is baker, *too.* You know why me love baker? Because he bake many cookies! And me **love** to *eat* cookies. Me eat these cookies NOW!

No, wait!
Cookies are for counting!

No!
Cookies for eating!

Counting!

Counting!

Eating!

Eating!

WAIT!

First I will count them, then you can eat them. One, two, three . . .

Yum. Yum. Yum. Uh, excuse me, would you mind (yum) counting a little (yum, yum) faster?

Egad! I see through my magnifying glass that these People in my Neighborhood are each missing something. They need a good detective.

What's Missing?

Aha! Here are the missing things. Can *you* cut them out and paste them where they belong?

ICE CREAM

U.S. MAIL

When I Grow Up
by Big Bird

When I grow up I'll drive a bus—
I'll let you honk the horn.
Or I could be a grocer—
And I'd sell peas and corn.

Or I could be a teacher—
I bet you'd learn a lot—
No, I think I'll be...a DANCER!
Oops—I think I'd better not.

On second thought, a carpenter
Is what I'd like the best—
I'd take a hammer, nails, and wood
And build a brand new nest.

Or...I could be a doctor—
And I'd make you feel all better.
Or I could be a mailman—
And I'd bring you a letter.

There are so many things to be—
It's really hard to choose.
But while I'm waiting to grow up...
I think I'll take a snooze.

What are you doing back here? Didn't I tell you to close the book and go away?

Well, since you are here, I might as well show you what I'm doing with these two old paper cups. You see, I'm the Grouch telephone man, and I'm making—

A GROUCH-O-PHONE!

First I poke a little hole in the bottom of each cup. Then I take this long piece of string and I stick an end through each hole, and I tie a fat knot in each end. That keeps the string from coming out.

Now watch this. I take one cup, and Maria here takes the other and stands far enough away so that the string is tight.

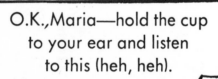

O.K., Maria—hold the cup to your ear and listen to this (heh, heh).

Are you ready?

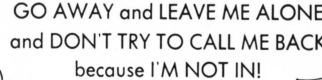

GO AWAY and LEAVE ME ALONE and DON'T TRY TO CALL ME BACK because I'M NOT IN!

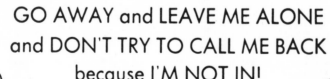

What you need:

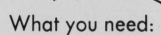

A long piece of string
2 paper cups
A pencil (for poking holes in the cups)
A nice GROUCHY temper!

FIRE! FIRE!

There's a fire in the hot dog cart. Help Fireman Ernie get to the fire so he can put it out.

Do you know what this chapter is all about,
Mommy? It is all about

FEELINGS

And do you know something
else, Mommy? I love you.

I love you,
too, Grover.
Now go to
sleep, dear.

I Used to Be Afraid

by Grover and Ernie

When I was little I used to be scared
Of being alone in the night.
I'd pull the blankets up over my head
And pray that the sky would get light...

But then my mommy sat by my bed
And said there was nothing to fear,
'Cause nothing scary went on in the night
And she and my daddy were near.

When I was little I used to be scared
Of taking a bath in the tub.
I thought when the water ran down the drain
That I would go with it...Glub-Glub.

But my old buddy Bert said,
"Come on, use your brain.
If you just take a look, you will see
That you NEVER could fit
through that very small drain!"

Now my tubby's where I love to be.

Do you want to have some fun? Then COLOR this

SAD CLOWN,

turn him UPSIDE DOWN, and what have you got?...

A HAPPY CLOWN!

Cookie Monster's
Surprise Cookies

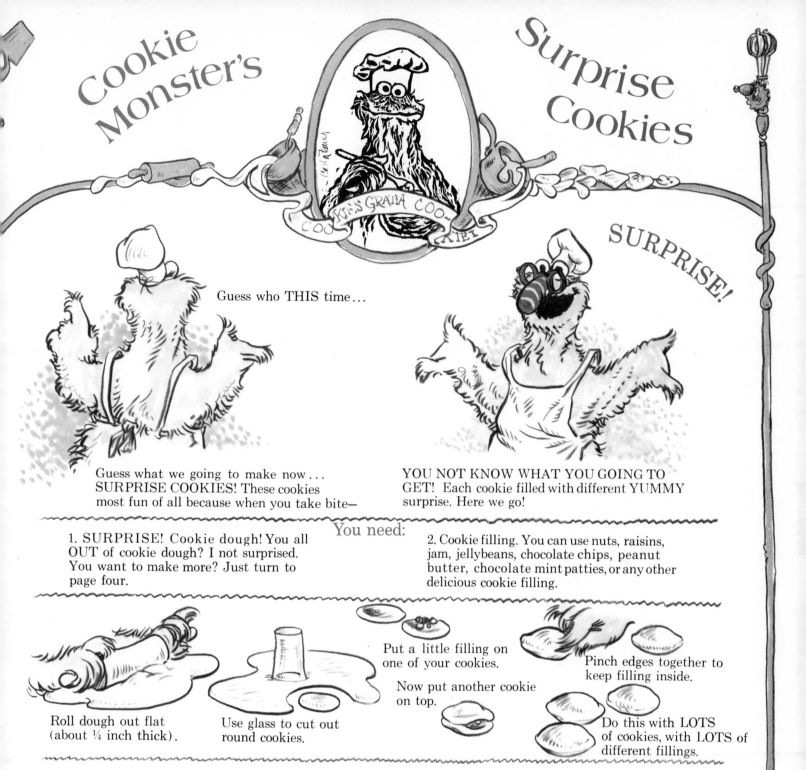

Guess who THIS time...

SURPRISE!

Guess what we going to make now...
SURPRISE COOKIES! These cookies
most fun of all because when you take bite—

YOU NOT KNOW WHAT YOU GOING TO
GET! Each cookie filled with different YUMMY
surprise. Here we go!

You need:

1. SURPRISE! Cookie dough! You all
OUT of cookie dough? I not surprised.
You want to make more? Just turn to
page four.

2. Cookie filling. You can use nuts, raisins,
jam, jellybeans, chocolate chips, peanut
butter, chocolate mint patties, or any other
delicious cookie filling.

Roll dough out flat
(about ¼ inch thick).

Use glass to cut out
round cookies.

Put a little filling on
one of your cookies.

Now put another cookie
on top.

Pinch edges together to
keep filling inside.

Do this with LOTS
of cookies, with LOTS of
different fillings.

Heat oven to 400 degrees. Put cookies on ungreased
cookie sheet. Put in oven and cook until LIGHTLY BROWNED. That will
take about...oh... eight minutes.

Now you ready for big surprise?
Cookies ALL LOOK ALIKE!
ME NOT KNOW *WHICH*
ONES HAVE *WHAT* INSIDE!
WHAT ME GOING TO DO?
Me guess me have to...

TASTE
THEM
ALL!

Hmmm. Me
think this
one choco-
late chip.
NOPE!
SURPRISE!
It peanut
butter. This
one is...
raisins?
NOPE!
SURPRISE!
It jellybean!
This one...

Oscar's Bad-Time Junk Band

INTRODUCING... LITTLE JERRY AND THE MONOTONES

Hey! I can't find my guitar—I feel MAD!

I can't find my drums—I feel SAD!

I can't find my maracas—I feel so BAD!

I think I left 'em on the bus—BOY, do I feel EMBARRASSED!

Oh, WOE!

WOE!

WOE!

WOE!

Listen! If you guys will promise to STOP THAT RACKET, I'll show you how to make some NEW instruments out of stuff from my famous trash collection.

Here's what you need to make a *guitar*:

A shoe box.

A cardboard tube from a roll of paper towels.

Large rubber bands (3 or 4).

A pencil.

Scissors.

Strong tape.

Here's how to make it

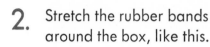

1. Cut a big hole in the middle of the lid of the box.

2. Stretch the rubber bands around the box, like this.

3. Put a pencil under the rubber bands . . . like this.

4. Tape the tube to one end of the box, like this.

   Your *Grouch Guitar* is ready to strum.

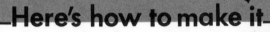

Here's what you need to make a *drum*:

An empty oatmeal box, or a coffee can with a plastic lid.

A longish loop of string.

Strong tape.

Paper and crayons.

Spoons or pencils.

Here's how to make it

1. Lay your long loop of string over the open top of the box, like this.

2. Tape the box top on tight, over the string.

3. Cut paper to fit around the box.

4. Decorate the paper with crayons.

5. Tape the paper around the box.

   Now put on your drum— and BEAT IT! (heh, heh)

Here's what you need to make *maracas*:

2 plastic spoons.

2 small containers with tops (you can use yogurt or sour cream cartons or small margarine or butter tubs).

Dried beans, small stones, macaroni— anything that will rattle.

Glue or tape.

Paper and crayons.

Here's how to make it

1. Cover the containers with decorated paper.

2. Glue or tape the paper in place.

   Punch a small hole in the bottom of each container.

3. Push the spoon handle through the hole, like this.

4. Put a handful of beans (or whatever) in the container.

5. Tape the tops on tight.

A Happy-Sad-Happy Sad-Happy Story

I have a story for you. It's about being HAPPY and being SAD. You can help me with your HAPPY—SAD masks. Whenever the people in the story are happy, hold up your HAPPY face mask and shout YAY! And when the story is sad, show the SAD side and say BOO-HOO! O.K., are you ready?

Once upon a time, in a little house near a little forest, there lived a little girl and a little boy. And they were very HAPPY.

But, one day, when the little boy went to the icebox to get something for lunch, all he could find was some liverwurst—and they both HATED liverwurst. And that made them very SAD.

"I have an idea," said the little girl. "Let's make liverwurst sandwiches and have a picnic. That will be fun!" And that idea made them very HAPPY.

YAY!

BOO HOO!

YAY!

So off they went into the forest to have their picnic. But no sooner had they spread out their picnic blanket, than a MONSTER jumped out from behind the trees. "LIVERWURST!" he yelled, and gobbled up all their sandwiches. This made the children very SAD.

When the monster saw how sad they were he reached into his pocket and pulled out a bag full of peanut butter and jelly sandwiches. "Here," he said. "My mommy made me peanut butter and jelly sandwiches for lunch and me HATE peanut butter and jelly. Me was so SAD until me saw your liverwurst. But that make me very HAPPY!"

BOO HOO!

FRITH

When the children saw the peanut butter and jelly sandwiches, that made them HAPPY, too.

...because this is the end of the story—and that makes *me* SAD.

YAY!

And so, that made everyone HAPPY —except for me...

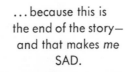

HOW TO MAKE A HAPPY-SAD MASK:
Just take a paper plate or a round piece of cardboard.

On one side draw a HAPPY face...

...On the other side draw a SAD face.

Take a paper towel tube and make a slit in the top. Then slip in your HAPPY—SAD face...and that's it.

Now are you HAPPY?

Greetings! It is **I, the Count.** Do you know why they call me **the Count?** Because I LOVE to *count* things. And do you know why I LOVE this chapter? Because it is the . . .

NUMBERS

chapter!

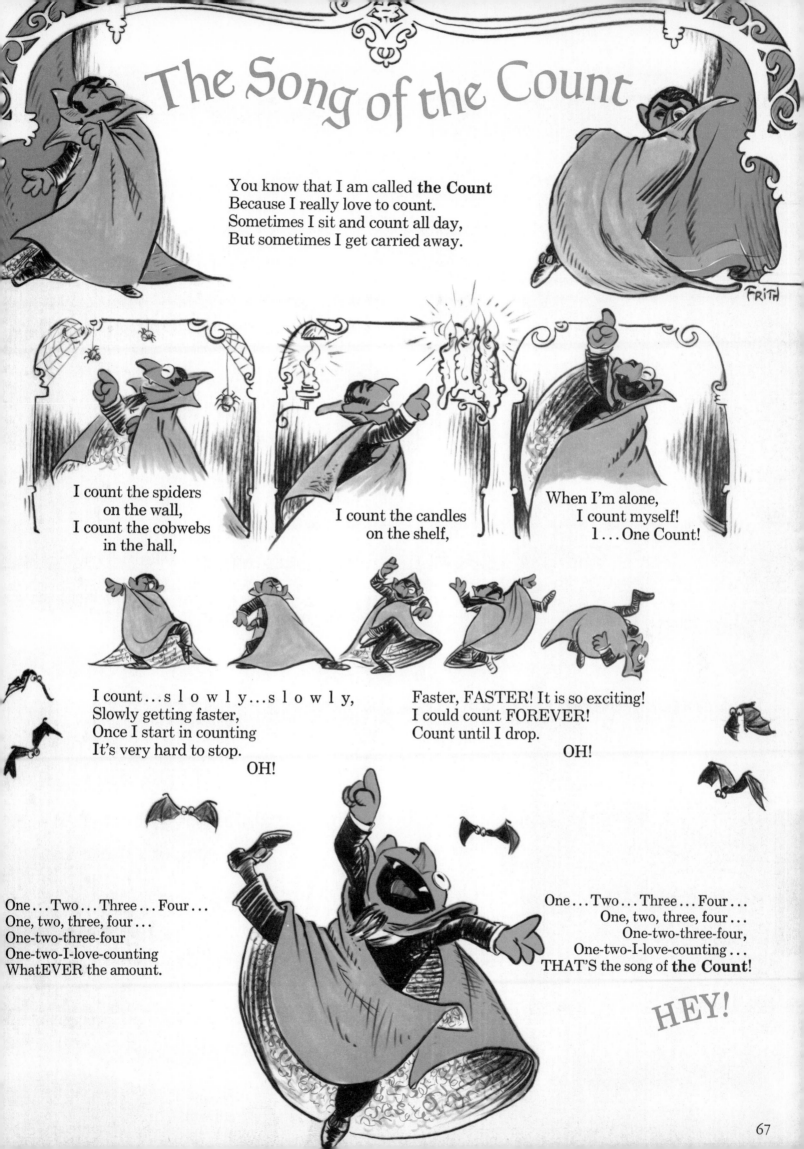

The Song of the Count

You know that I am called **the Count**
Because I really love to count.
Sometimes I sit and count all day,
But sometimes I get carried away.

I count the spiders
on the wall,
I count the cobwebs
in the hall,

I count the candles
on the shelf,

When I'm alone,
I count myself!
1...One Count!

I count...s l o w l y...s l o w l y,
Slowly getting faster,
Once I start in counting
It's very hard to stop.

OH!

Faster, FASTER! It is so exciting!
I could count FOREVER!
Count until I drop.

OH!

One...Two...Three...Four...
One, two, three, four...
One-two-three-four
One-two-I-love-counting
WhatEVER the amount.

One...Two...Three...Four...
One, two, three, four...
One-two-three-four,
One-two-I-love-counting...
THAT'S the song of **the Count**!

HEY!

Bert's 10 Collections

Ernie! Ernie! Come quickly. I've finally finished my ten collections. Now I have a separate collection for each of the numbers from one to ten. Oh! It's so exciting!

That's great, Bert! Let me see!

1 brick

2 brown paper bags

3 sponges

4 hats with little feathers on them

5 rulers

6 combs

7 pink erasers

8 wax bananas

9 paper clips

10 bottle caps

You see, I finally finished it when I found the Figgy-Fizz top for my bottle cap collection. That makes TEN, and . . . Ernie?

Ernie? Oh, wake up, Ernie.

Oscar's Bowling Contest

"Hey, everybody, come here. I've got something to show you!"

"I just won the Annual Grouch Bowling Contest. Let me show you my amazing style!"

"Luis, you set up those milk cartons on the sidewalk."

"Susan, hand me that big wad of tin foil. Now—watch this!"

"Oh, Oscar! Your...uh... beautiful trophy is broken!"

"Hey, will you look at that? That's terrific! Why didn't I think of that before?"

What you need:

6 empty milk cartons

A ball of tin foil

Paper and pencil for keeping score

How to play:

1. Set up cartons like this...

2. Stand about ten steps away from the cartons.

3. Each player takes a turn trying to knock down the cartons with the tin foil ball.

4. Count how many cartons you've knocked down and write it on the scorecard.

5. After each turn, set up the cartons for the next player.

6. The player who has knocked down the most cartons after three turns WINS!

Ernie Buys a 12

One morning, as Ernie was walking home from Mr. Hooper's store with a box of eggs for breakfast, he heard a mysterious voice...

Hey, kid... c'mere!

Who...ME?

Ssshhhhhh. I got somp'n for ya. How'd ya like to buy a number **12**?

A number **12**? Gee, why do I need a number **12**?

Ssshhhh. Well, I see you've got a dozen eggs there. D'you know how many eggs there are in a dozen?

Why... NO!

12! There're **12** eggs in a dozen. Next time y'wanna know how many eggs in a dozen, ya just take out your number **12** and there it is.

Oh! That's nifty! I'll take it! How much is it?

Tell ya what I'm gonna do. Ya look like a nice kid. I'm gonna trade ya this be-yoo-tiful number **12** for just one dozen eggs.

Oh, kind sir! How can I ever thank you. Now whenever I forget how many eggs are in my... uh... hey, wait a minute... uh... kind sir?

Hey, Bert, how'd you like a fried number **12** for breakfast?

10
Ten
tiny toy tops.

9
Nine
nice nose nests.

1
One
wobbly wombat.

Two
tweeting
Twiddlebugs.
2

Big Bird's Beak Breakers

I have a beak-breaker for every number from one to ten. See if you can say each one three times quickly.

3
Three
thick thumb
thimbles.

8
Eight
great grape
graters.

Oh, dear!
I don't think my beak will ever be the same!

4
Four
fake fairies
fall flat.

7
Seven
snickering snails.

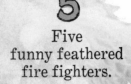

5
Five
funny feathered
fire fighters.

6
Six
she-seals sell seashells.

With **ONE** egg cup and four pipe cleaners you can make a darling spider . . .

And with **TWO** egg cups and three pipe cleaners and a cork you can make an adorable camel . . .

you can hang your bat with a rubber band

And with **THREE** egg cups and no pipe cleaners you can make a lovable bat . . .

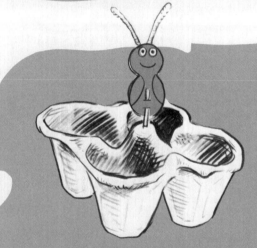

And with **FOUR** egg cups and one pipe cleaner you can make an EXCITING COUNTING GAME called Twiddlywinks.

TWIDDLYWINKS

HOW TO MAKE IT
1. Make a Twiddlebug out of paper or cardboard. (Use a pipe cleaner for the feelers and draw on the eyes, mouth, and wings.)
2. Cut two slots in the Twiddlebug and put a toothpick through the slots.
3. Cut out four connecting sections of an egg carton and stick the Twiddlebug toothpick in the center.

HOW TO PLAY IT
1. Collect 10 pennies or buttons to use as tokens.
2. Put the Twiddle-cups on a table or on the floor, about two feet from the players.
3. Each player takes a turn and tries to toss the 10 tokens into the cups.
4. The player who gets the most tokens into the Twiddle-cups wins.

Frith

And with **FIVE** egg cups and two pipe cleaners you can make this BEAUTIFUL caterpillar . . .

. . . Isn't it exciting? *Five* marvelous toys!

Well, I have something exciting for you. **ONE** mop and **ONE** bucket and I'd like to see that **ONE** mess cleaned up before I count to **THREE**!

Start counting! Start counting!

BODY PARTS

Ernie's Guessing Game

Hey, Bert! Come here. I've got a terrific guessing game.

Oh, good, Ernie. I love guessing games. What do I do first?

Well, you see, I've put a lot of things on the table here. Now I'm going to blindfold you and hand you one of the things and YOU have to guess what it is. O.K.?

But ERNIE! How can I tell what it is if I can't see it?

Oh, easy, Bert. You can feel it with your HANDS, or smell it with your NOSE, or listen to it with your EARS, or taste it with your TONGUE. Here, try this one.

This is going to be fun, Ernie. Hmmmm, this feels sort of smooth with lumps on it. It smells kind of . . . SOAPY? It doesn't make ANY noise . . .

SQUEEZE it, Bert!

Why, Ernie! It's your RUBBER DUCKIE! Hey, that was fun. Now it's your turn.

QUACK QUACK

Hmmmm. This feels kind of round . . . with little bumps on it. It smells . . . nice. It doesn't make any noise. Maybe I should TASTE it. Hmmm . . . what could it be? I'd better try another one. Nope . . . I'll try one more. I can't figure it out. I'll just try another . . . and another . . . and . . .

Ernie— don't you know what it is YET?

Bert, I think I have it! Those were the chocolate-chip cookies you bought for our dessert tonight! They were DELICIOUS!

ERNIE!!! I give up!

If you'd like to play this game, here are some things you can use. And remember—no peeking!

Ball	Book
Bell	Orange
Clock	Spoon, Fork
Keys	Toys
Cup	Cookies
Apple	Pencil
Potato	Crayon
Tomato	Carrot

80

Luis's Fingerprint Pictures

Hola, Big Bird. I have a great idea for your Busy Book. Let's make fingerprint pictures.

Oh! That sounds like fun. How do you do that, Luis?

Well, first we have to make some fingerprint paint. We need

½ cup of flour

¼ cup of water

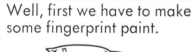

Mix them up and add

½ cup of liquid detergent or liquid laundry starch.

Then add food coloring or poster paint

and mix it *all* up together.

Now get some paper, and you're ready to make fingerprint pictures.

When they dry, you can draw faces on them.

But, Luis . . .

Just a minute, Big Bird. You can make fingerprint designs, or . . .

Well, what is it Big Bird?

I don't have fingers, like you! I'm a bird, and . . .

WAIT! I bet I could make FOOT prints though. Let me see . . .

¡Oh, qué desorden!

I have this poem here about body parts.
My friends are going to show you what they are.

Ankle, Shoulder, Knee
by Big Bird

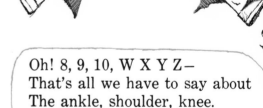

Oh! A knee is kinda roundish, like an orange or an egg;
You'll find it sticking out, right in the middle of your leg.
It bends right in the middle when you want to run or jump;
It's a funny kinda, lumpy kinda, knobby kinda bump.

Oh! A B C D – 1, 2, 3,
Let's all sing a song about a knee!

Oh! A shoulder is the joint that's at the top part of your arm,
And everybody's got 'em, in the city or the farm.
It's so useful when you want to wave hello or wave good-bye,
And wiggling it up and down is easy if you try.

Oh! A B C – When you are older,
Hope you'll remember this song about a shoulder.

Oh! An ankle can be found at the beginning of your foot,
And when you're getting dressed, it's in the sock that it is put.
An ankle is important if you want to dance or run,
And if anybody kicks you there, it isn't any fun.

Oh! A B C – A jinkle and a jankle,
It's hard to find a rhyme
For a silly word like ankle.

When you think about your body
And you think of all its parts,
Don't only think of eyes and ears,
Of noses, mouths, and hearts...
Think of the parts that move and bend,
That help both you and me
To walk and run and jump and play—
The ankle, shoulder, knee.

Oh! 8, 9, 10, W X Y Z –
That's all we have to say about
The ankle, shoulder, knee.
Wheeee!

Cookie Monster's
Cookie Faces

Guess who! Right you are! It me again...
old COOKIE MONSTER! And this time me
got WONDERFUL recipe for you. Me love it
because me make FACES of all my friends.
You want to do it, too? O.K., me tell you how.

You need
1. Cookie dough (you can make more if you need
it — just look at page four).
2. Cookie decorations, like raisins, or jellybeans,
or small hard candies; sprinkles, or frosting, or nuts.

Sprinkle flour on cloth and roll out your
dough on it (about ¼ inch thick).

Now cut out face shapes and peel away
extra dough, like this...

Now decorate them.   Raisins make good hair and eyes. Jellybean make
VERY tasty nose. Here are some of
my COOKIE FRIENDS...

ERNIE
Red
jellybean
nose.

BERT
Orange
jellybean
nose.

GROVER
Pink
jellybean nose.
And sprinkles
make him look
fuzzy.

SUSAN and GORDON
Peanuts make good noses
for people.

Now heat oven to 400 degrees,
put in cookies, and wait six to
eight minutes. Oh, boy! Me can
hardly wait to have my friends
for dinner!

Oh, dear! I was going to color in all these pictures of my friends, but somehow all their bodies got MIXED UP. Please cut the page on the dotted lines and help me get them back together again.

J. Mathieu

J. Mathieu

Oh, thanks!
Now we can do
some coloring.

Hi! It's us—BIG Bird
and LITTLE Bird—and
we're here to bring you the...

OPPOSITES

chapter

Tall and Short Poem

by Big Bird and Little Bird

I wish I were as big as you,
I wish that I were tall.
I'm tired of being overlooked,
I'm tired of being small.

If I were tall, I'd stand up straight
And reach the highest shelf,
And if my toy was stuck up there
I could get it by myself!

I wish that I were short like you,
I wish that I were small.
I tower over everyone,
I'm tired of being tall.

If I were short it would be fun,
I'd never bump my head,
And my feet would not get chilly
'Cause they stick out of my bed.

But sometimes when you're trying to hide,
It's better to be small.

And being tall is not so bad
When playing basketball.

So maybe when we think it out,
What's really best by far
Is finding out what's good about
Being the way you are.

This is Roosevelt here
to bring you good cheer!
I've got a NEW game
and this is its name.

HOT and COLD

Can you dig it?

O.K.
Here's how to play . . .
Get something small—
like a button or a penny. Send your friends out of
the room, and hide it. When you're ready, call your
friends back into the room. Now they have to find it.
They ask you, "Is it near the TV?" If they're close
you say, "You're getting hot." They say, "Is it
under the rug?" If they're further away you
say, "You're getting cold." You keep playing
until someone guesses where it is. Then
that person gets to hide
it next.

MUST be in
the goldfish
bowl!

When you're
hot, you're
hot!

Cookie Monster's Big and Little Cookies

COOKIES GRATIA COO... ...ATIE!

You ready for this? This EASIEST recipe of all — you only make two cookies!

A GREAT **BIG** COOKIE like this one...

and a cute, ADORABLE, teeny LITTLE cookie like this one.

FRITH

You need:
1. COOKIE DOUGH—for this one maybe you better make some more (look at page four).
2. Chocolate chips and crispy rice cereal.

First, roll out dough ¼ inch thick. Now cut out cute LITTLE cookie. O.K.? Now take REST OF DOUGH and cut out **BIGGEST** COOKIE you can fit on cookie sheet. O.K.? Sprinkle chocolate chips and cereal on cookies to make them even MORE delicious. Now put in oven and cook six to eight minutes at 400 degrees.

While you waiting for cookies to cook, you can *color in* PICTURES OF ME and my cookies! That is fun... but it even more fun eating cookies when they're done!

Hey, Mr. Hooper, do you have any extra paper bags? Maria and I want to show the kids how to make Front and Back Masks.

Why, yes, David. Here they are. But tell me, what's a Front and Back Mask?

O.K., Mr. Hooper. But first, do you have a pair of scissors we could use?

Here they are, David. Now—what is a Front and Back Mask?

Just a minute, Mr. Hooper. Do you have some crayons we can borrow?

Sure, sure, sure, Maria. NOW will you tell me what a Front and Back Mask is?

Just as soon as you give us some yarn and sticky tape, Mr. Hooper.

O.K.! O.K.! Here they are. NOW . . . will you PLEASE tell me . . . WHAT *IS* A FRONT AND BACK MASK?

Here it is, Mr. Hooper! Now no one will know who you are.

Oh, hi, Mr. Blooper. Gee, you're looking very well today. Did you get a haircut or something?

HOW TO MAKE A FRONT AND BACK MASK

1. Find a paper bag big enough to fit over your head.

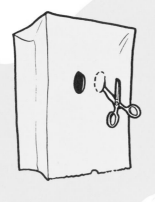

2. Cut two holes in the bag for eyes.

If you want to, you can cut holes for your nose and mouth, too.

3. Draw a funny face on the front of the mask.

FRONT BACK

FRONT BACK

STICK YARN ON WITH GLUE OR STICKY-TAPE!

4. Stick yarn or string on the bag for hair.

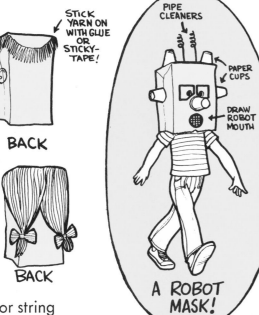

PIPE CLEANERS

PAPER CUPS

DRAW ROBOT MOUTH

A ROBOT MASK!

YOU ARE SO CUTE!

If you really want to surprise people, draw a face on the front, and *another* face on the back. Your friends won't know if you're coming or going.

Oh, yeah? Well, with the mask I'm making . . .

. . . people will know if *I'm* coming or going . . .

. . . I'm *ALWAYS* going!

Sherlock Hemlock
in
The Case of the Lost Lunch

Boo-hoo!

E-Gad! A bird in distress! What is the matter, Little Bird?

Oh, Mr. Sherlock Hemlock, sir, my friend Big Bird invited me to his nest for a delicious birdseed lunch, and I don't know how to get there. And I'm getting VERY hungry.

Never fear, Little Bird. I, Sherlock Hemlock, the World's Greatest Detective, will help you find the way to Big Bird's nest.

Oh, look! There's a trail of birdseed on the ground. Maybe Big Bird dropped it on the way home from Mr. Hooper's store.

E-Gad! A trail of birdseed! Perhaps Big Bird dropped it on his way home from Mr. Hooper's store. If we follow it, we may find our way to Big Bird's nest.

Look! Mr. Hemlock... (munch, munch)

MUNCH! MUNCH!

The birdseed leads...

(gobble, gobble) UNDER this fence.

(smack, gulp) Look—OVER the bridge...

(crunch, yum) He must have gone DOWN this hill...

(munch, crunch) and UP these stairs...

(yum, yum) and IN this door...

(yum, yum) and OUT that door... and there he is!

Oh, Little Bird! I'm so glad you got here! But I have terrible news for you. There was a *hole* in my bag of birdseed and it all *leaked* out. And now there's nothing left for lunch....

That's O.K., Big Bird. I'm not very hungry anyway.

E-GAD!

HELP LITTLE BIRD FIND HIS WAY TO BIG BIRD'S NEST

UNDER THE FENCE

OVER THE BRIDGE

DOWN THE HILL

UP THE STAIRS

IN THE DOOR

OUT THE DOOR